A Hat

by Tristan Horrom
illustrated by Yvette Banek

Decodable 2

Mc
Graw
Hill
Education

Bothell, WA • Chicago, IL • Columbus, OH • New York, NY

MHEonline.com

Send all inquiries to:
McGraw-Hill Education
8787 Orion Place
Columbus, OH 43240

ISBN: 978-0-02-145302-3
MHID: 0-02-145302-0

Printed in the United States of America.

7 8 9 LCR 25 24 23

Pat, a map!

To the map!

Pat at a map

Pat taps.

To the hat!

Pat at a hat